Novel

Cati Porter

BAMBOO DART PRESS

LOS ANGELES † NEW YORK † LONDON † MELBOURNE

Novel by Cati Porter

ISBN: 978-1-947240-45-2
eISBN: 978-1-947240-46-9

Cover artwork by Dennis Callaci
Chapbook design and layout by Mark Givens

For information:
Bamboo Dart Press
chapbooks@bamboodartpress.com

Bamboo Dart Press 020

Pelekinesis
www.pelekinesis.com

BAMBOO DART PRESS
www.bamboodartpress.com

SHRIMPER
www.shrimperrecords.com

Other Books by Cati Porter

Contents

As Margaret napped through the apocalypse

on the apartment couch near the window
a stampede of saddle shoes outside
trampled the marigolds
as businesspersons ran
from offices eating footlong hot dogs
and slurping slushies
being chased by giant staplers

An umbrella deep as a cloud is throwing shade

Cantilevered

Somewhere in the house she has been
hoarding a bridge for safe keeping

in case the earth should need an extension
the cords are the connectors

everything is electrified and still
the room is dark the bottom flat

with the shifting of a mound
of catalogues jewel tones ring

the hearth walls are held up by strangers
& we all hold our positions as

architects design the elements
to withstand the structure

the fact remains that stories contain
truth lies in the balance

Because the Dead Cannot Tie Their Shoes

they wear flip-flops, chanclas, zories, thongs—
whatever you have learned to call them.

Knobby toes rise up on either side
of the divide, invite in the stones:
rocky beaches, asphalt shrapnel, gutters
of broken glass. The dead roam
among us, restless, seeking
blisters, cuts, anything
to make them feel again.
The dead dream
of suckling juicy lemons
with an ulcerated tongue, drizzle
alcohol in paper cuts, rub soap
and sunscreen in their eyes.

Ghostly dust bunnies nestle on
the closet floor, listen as like-new lace-ups
lament with their brethren about their lot,
consider the difference between *can't* and *won't*.

Richard Garcias Are Everywhere

CP: Richard, why are there two of you here on Facebook?
RG: There are several of us authorized to be Richard Garcia
       in this quadrant.

At first there was some ambiguity.
I could never be certain that it wasn't
the same Richard Garcia I'd seen
in multiple places the same day,
until once I saw two in one supermarket,
shopping separate aisles. Recently
I spotted several in a used car lot
vying to purchase a single Powell Plymouth.
Last week a number of them went
door to door in the neighborhood,
peddling books by Neruda like evangelists.
Yesterday they marched from the Library
of Congress to the library downtown
carrying signs and flags emblazoned
with quatrains. CNN first reported
sightings in cities across the state,
then the continent, then the globe.
Richard Garcias were carrying
torches all through the night,
reciting poems as they marched.
Richard Garcias in South Carolina,
Tennessee, Wisconsin, California,

demanding the rights of poets everywhere:
Give us poetry or give us death!
Only then did everyone begin wondering,
*Who is this "Richard Garcia"? And why
are there so many of him?* Some wondered,
Which is the real Richard Garcia? as if
that mattered. If you listen, an eerie
whooshing can be heard as *El Zapato*
flies toward The One True Richard Garcia,
powering up his army of Richard Garcias,
each but the original implanted with a device
to thwart the inevitable shoe.

Lazarus in the Bookstore

Lazarus was alive, and then he wasn't.
A clutch of books fell from his arms as he
folded. A crowd gathered, took out cell phones.

No one believes anymore, He thinks, browsing
the spirituals in which "He" is referred
to as merely myth, not even historical.

But real is a matter of faith, He thinks
as even He begins to wonder as
no one gathers to wash his sandaled feet.

At His command, Lazarus rolls over
and the crowds disperse. Later some may claim
"miracle" but in fact no one took notice.

Among the books purchased by Him that day:
"How to Raise a Saint." Nearby in Children's
an angelic toddler is raising hell.

Folding Dave

Today the filming begins and I am anxious
because Dave is anxious. He is drinking
his hot tea through a straw. His tea is spiked
with the tears of my grandmother, which
I will use to starch his collarbone, his knees.
The camera begins rolling so it is now
that I must explain again to Dave why
we are doing this, that it is for the children,
for posterity, for generations to come, to see
how it is done. I gesture toward the table
and Dave hops up onto the edge, knees
buckled, dress shoes kicking the chilled air.
It is best to fold when it's cold. I lift Dave's
knees up and onto the exam table, lay
him back, and while prone I slip my hand
beneath his buttocks, slide to mid thigh, lift
upward. His shoes flat toward the ceiling fan,
legs stiff, I begin the first fold, legs to chest,
one foot over each shoulder. I press
everything into place. I smooth his thighs
and the backs of his knees until they are flat.
I begin the next fold. The cameraman zooms
in: I fold Dave in half again. Dave's limbs
yield. He is now compact enough
to fit in a drawer, a wheeled suitcase,
a shoulder holster, at the ready
to be brought out again
whenever only a Dave will do.
Everyone needs a Dave.

Disarming Sue

Isn't she charming?
Each word is loaded
with intent. See
Sue. She is dangerous.
Her phrases drip,
weaponized. To
disarm her, first,
ask her to dance,
then twist her arms
until you hear a snap.
Her arms will slip right out
of her sleeves. Armless,
she can take her place
in line with the other girls,
waiting to be fitted
with a safer, more
compliant pair.

Self-Portrait in the Kitchen as the Wife without Hands

I am that woman who on all fours licks
the baseboards, each spot of spilt grease on the
floor rubbed up with an elbow, the stump of
a wrist. The pots gleam. I drain pasta by
slipping pot holders up my arms, tipping
with my chin, the steam pinking my cheeks.
At the table I use my teeth to write poems
in beet ink, build elaborate trapezes
that I use to swing above the stove by
my knees. I don't know what any of this
means except that when the call comes to
tell me that the ship is in the driveway and
there are pirates on the lawn, I imagine
myself fighting off the hordes with a spoon
wedged beneath my tongue. The counter
is covered with selkies, with mermen.
The carrots and onions conspire in the
cupboard to remake what I have lost,
rooting for me, but I love what I have become.

"Cooking With the Women You Have Loved"

Thank you for joining us. Tonight we are cooking with
women. But not just any women; the women you have loved.
First up is your first crush. (Canned applause) Here, the chef
drizzles a vial of her sweaty playground essence and swirls it
into the bathwater that will form the broth. Whose crush, you
ask? Yours, sir, in the third row. (A gentleman gestures in a
pointing fashion to himself to indicate mock astonishment.)
Next we have your mother. Here is an anxiety-filled bouillon
cube made from all those nights she waited up for you, salted
with her tears of regret for not making you adhere to your
studies. Here, the chef drops the cube into the mixture and it
softens and fizzles like a bath bomb until it's one with the wa-
ter. Now we will add your first love, that girl who begged you
not to drop out of college. Here, we add the meat to the broth,
on the bone. How did we get it? Don't ask. No, don't get up
sir, please, sit back down. No, of course it isn't really her. Now
we chop, chop, chop the carrots, celery, potatoes, drop a hand-
ful of pearl onions, and let that simmer until done. For the
main dish, we give you (drumroll please) your ex-wife, yes, the
one who just left you just today, because you scolded her once
again for using the word "just" just a bit too much. Please,
stay seated. Don't mind the men firmly pressing down on your
shoulders to keep you in your seat. It's important that you
remain still right now. For all our sakes. Here she is! See her
squirming as she is brought onstage. It's just an act, you know,
no one ever really gets hurt. Yes, those men are indeed holding

a very large roasting bag. See them gently slip
it over her head. Yes, she did volunteer for this. No, it's
quite alright. Please, sir, don't close your eyes, even
as she struggles to climb into the bag. Remember:
She chose this. You did too.

Recipe for Failure

First, gather ingredients:

One bowl instead of two
Six eggs (two of which are cracked)
Too much flour
Not enough milk
A fork for a wooden spoon
        Kenny G

Add all to the bowl
        Stir. Cry
over the batter, which, unlike
in *Like Water for Chocolate*,
does not convey any
magical properties

Pour into a pie pan
Pop it in, forget
to preheat
        Sit. Wait

Tender

Fork it, and meat falls off the bone—
submerged in the pot, scenting
the kitchen with its soapy stock

unstirred, unsettled in summer's afterglow.
Light a candle & watch the wick
blacken, its watery blue flame.

Heat nibbles the edges of the pot.
Touch it! Prove that the body is an object
that dissolves into music — raspberries
of a rolling boil, thick rhythm of a spoon.

In the forgery of memory, the recipe
has not yet been clipped, nor the hunter's bullet;
the hunter's hunger un-satiated.

Death has not yet left her house
with a rifle in mind; the white wick, un-darkened;
the pot, heavy on its hook, still gleaming.

Dear Deer

I spotted him in the forest
nuzzling the hunter.

It was as though he knew
Death was coming, and rather
than sprint away, he approached
her first. When he tilted
his head, she pressed the muzzle
firmly against his temple,
and he eased into it as one
might ease oneself into a chilly
stream. I watched as he toppled
onto leaf litter. The hunter
lifted him, carried him
to her truck like one might carry
a slumbering child to bed.

When it began to snow,
I lay down where he had lain.
The blanket was still warm.

Death's "Daily Affirmations for Confidence and Success"

1. I am confident in my ability to transition the living to the dead.
2. I give myself permission to do my job as I must without remorse.
3. I am *good* at this job. I've been told I'm a "natural."
4. So what if I've been passed over for higher office? It's their loss.
5. Next time, I will not be intimidated! I will ask for that raise!
6. When I'm feeling down, I give myself permission to wear my fuzzy purple slippers. Purple makes me feel good!
6. Repeat: It is never my fault. It is never my decision.
7. It's acceptable to arrive early to give them the impression they were able to negotiate for that "extra" day. Win/win!
8. Accept that drink! Accept that bubble bath!
9. Never tell them why.
10. Don't forget to turn off the lights.

I Will Miss You When I'm Dead

There is an appeal to dying, or so I am told.
First, you no longer have to register your car.
If you want to streak across the field during
playoff season, no one will stop you.
You can prank your neighbors and friends
like, *Who moved that potted plant?*
Glasses become irrelevant.
And noses. And fingers. So what you're
now eligible to attend the post-corporeal
weekly square dance and potluck?
Hell, you might even enjoy it.
But you only die once. And there's no one
I'd rather die beside than you.
Until then living will have to do.

Supernova, Or the End is Just the Beginning

We are blue, the sky only reflection.
Orange blossoms sugar ordinary
air, blunt sharp grass. We snails scale garden walls,
proceed inevitably, barnacles
on the of arrow of time. Neil and Carl have
shot us across the Cosmos on a raft,
universe peeling back, our craft fading
to dust, disintegrating in the sun
while we bicker and make love. The field is
the open-ended blur of the now, each
of us stemmed, upturned toward. Rootless, rooting,
we soften. One kiss and all reduces
to choreography. Heart-stars erupt
in a profusion. Elsewhere other stars
            are burning, burning.

Evergreen

The checkerboard boy unfolds before my eyes
the way a straw-wrapper snake takes shape.

Soon we are sipping chocolate egg creams
in companionable silence.

He and his saddle shoes match the linoleum.
Sure, he's a square, but so am I.

We hold our breath so that
this moment may last a lifetime.

We know by morning
he will again transmogrify.

Soon the mood downshifts
and Barbra Streisand makes us cry.

Frost was right.
We hold our breath all through the night.

Lofty

Engirdled by twining vine, rope threaded
through fruit, then back around him: seems secure?
He will never go hungry, this growing boy
trailing garlands of apples strung thickly on a line.

He is perched, shirtless, in the convoluted tree,
flushed and unassailable, long legs
dangled and tangling; his rolling curls gleam.

At least he has his books, I think, though
they too are out on a limb, peculiar
as the nearby turtle suspended by a vine mid-air.
The world of day jobs and offices, beneath him:
once I believed he might make a career
in architecture or automotive sciences.

A nearby branch balances an adjacent sailing ship
which tips, pours its sea onto a cobbled ball
strung up between trees. Ornamental. Decorated
with fruit and flora; the heads of incurious birds.

Red-bodied tree frogs observe in silence
From the scene, I discern but do not say:
Fruit rots. Wood decays. Rope frays. Bodies burn.
Given time, this and other lessons he will learn.

In Spite of Her Reservations,

She plunges the spade
into the soil, snap
roots beneath the blade,
lunges into, leans
away. The flat of
it displaces earth,
unearths the knot which
she then gently lifts,
taps, knocks free, the roots
puddling like hair.
Her soles sink into
the muck, until she
is sunk. The quick has
risen up. It's hard
to tell. All she knows
is the spade clings to
her the way a child
clings to any hand
when danger is near.

The Door in the Forest

I'm walking in the forest and I can't find you
though the trees are sparse as thoughts,
the forest floor low and soft and un-concealing
Every forest has an entrance, even this,
and I walked through that door once to find
only that nothing changes once inside.
Child, witness the way the mind flattens
until it can be unrolled like a featherbed—
Child of the matted pine: wake up.
Lichen child, feather child, ghost child, mine,
the threshold is an illusion, watch your step.
Bristling roots interleave chapters of soil.
The ever-after jaws like a dream; the forest,
forever, longs to swallow you, as I do,
like a remedy, would dissolve you, if it could —
You must resolve to keep on walking.

Revival

In the garden there grows an argument
beneath the apples, apocalyptic
hydrangeas exploding into blue fumes,
roses ripe as a picked-at scab,
the salt-studded path burbling
with snails' fresh foam.

In the garden there it grows,
behind the toolshed, between
the tines of the rustled rake, the mucked
wheelbarrow, the brown thick of the shovel,
the garden's profusion of chokecherries,
raspberries, amid the ground's sullied gold.

In the garden, a home to worm and bone,
beetle hulls, chassis of vehicles protruding
from the mulch, busts and torsos
marbling in the sun, and shining,
wheat chafing the thighs of those who rise here—
whole groves of us breaking the soil, cracking beneath the sun.

In the garden we grow, impertinent weeds,
whistling reeds, diseased trunks, a whole litany
of assertions; electric poles tilting, telephone wires
wringing silence from the clearing, reawakening
the chiming and chirruping birds, the sunflowers
performing their yellow mysteries.

In the garden, a blunt elbow, an artist's wrist,
a pubic bone, a rush of hair, a globe
glistening on the dismissed surface,
leaves greening and unrolling their deep need.
What goes to seed in this holy erasure
grows, the burning bush extinguished.

In the garden, this awe, this expectation
of rough beauty, this supple white hope, raw
and clinking in the air, the tossed coin's messy
aspirations; this disaster, a revival;
the gloss and sheen of love
like vaseline, lubricating our fall.

Pluck

Sisters glimmered on the tree like gemstones,
like lanterns, bright with the knowledge that they

could soon be picked, the garden in darkness
without them. The sisters hung on by their

necks, by their nails, even as winds knocked red
bodies against. They evaded harvest,

spurned even eligible suitors.
The sisters did fall, as they must, but held

on longest of their kin, determined to
forever after steer their own fortune.

The Apple-Polisher

She sells her apples to the highest bidder
at market. She comes home with pennies
in her pocket: freedom. The market corners
her apples the way a page comes to a point
at its corners, sharp and full of unearned
wisdom. Someone somewhere is always
polishing the apples for sale, and they get
shinier by the moment. Sometimes she throws
the apple of discord into the crowd
and watches them fight over the fruits
of her labor. Fruits are always borne
of women, she knows. She carries them
in a satchel. She clutches them. Eve knew
even as she drew down her first bite
that all children eventually perish. Drosophila
hover over the windfall. Every fleshy fruit
is derived of an ovary, with child. She adores
the process, not the product. Her apples cry
at being sent to market, but she can only
bear so much. They are too sweet. There are
those who would not partake of her apples
if they knew where they came from. They too
were her apples once, now seeded into tree.
Her calyx aches with every bite of their bitter butter.

A Gold Nothing and a Silver Wait-a-While

I spin you gold
a thread so fine
it makes your teeth
ache from that which
may be thrown across
that which is woven
to be fed through
the story meaning there
is always an apparatus
nothing being spun from
nothing for often something
with enough slivered silver
waiting can be made
of the loose ends
that will be beautiful
or at least useless

The Proper Care and Housing of Stories

I keep mine in a paddock.
When I take them out, I hold them close
to the body like warm laundry.
They squirm and wriggle and try to break free.

The stories sometimes push through
the fence, the one that I use to contain them.
Other times, I deliberately leave open the gate a smidge—
they think they are escaping, but there is always
the horizon to rein them in.

Sometimes I take them to the beach, scoop
out a trough just big enough to hold them
—about the size of a bathtub, so they can stretch—
and I gently set them in. I draw
pictograms in the sand
and together we watch
the waves obscure them.
The stories like that. It reminds them.

Sometimes I take my stories to the woods
to abandon them because
they are a bother, these stories,
but they always they find their way back
and when they arrive
I greet them
as though I never meant for them to leave.

They are so predictable, my stories.
I always know where they are going
until they emerge from my neighbor's garage
where a dismantled Mustang
has been replaced
by a horse made up
of sugar cubes.

The Fish on the Floor

are bleating, cerulean-fringed
& bulb-bellied.

Together we share the stairwell.
I swim the risers, up and down around them,
while they, fixed, contemplate the ceiling,
kindly almost-ghosts, wiving
the walls that rise unaware around them.

What are these banked fish
that flounder for air. Fill me with their kind
of breathing. Belly me up and hold me
to the sky, featherless and free—
falling to jelly the ground.

I float them in the pool.
They do not swim.

I cannot save them.

Postcards from the Bottom of the Pool

1.

The water is clear   I can see   sky as I lay on my back   eyes
open   to the layered blues   the trees   appear translucent
from here   my hands too when I fan   my fingers   like pale
fronds   feathered hair   a drain pipe song   long going down
and I am heavy   waiting I breathe in   and out sprout gills
oh where is my   seal fur suit   my body a glass   filling   I can
no longer   fell out   from the I'm   the last you know   please
what   is this   lighter as I am   going down   mailed the postal
carrier is a wet   how will you ever   read it   do do   can you
do you see it   can you see   can you see

2.

I have come to look for you but here looks break open like a
geode. My feet bleed as I walk across like a barefoot explorer,
plumes of red fanning out like wings at my heels. I bring you
my last best coat, spread it across the puddle, but how to spare
you from getting wet. That sound — singing — I hear your
voice weaving a trail through water, muffling and amplify-
ing, can't make out but I know you and reach down, touch the
drain, pull up strands of hair

3.

I see you   waking into this   dreaming   your heavy boots

shuffling   across   snorkel verticalling up   through
into   air   that reeks   here I am   here I lie   just beneath
you and   maybe when I say pool I mean ocean mean
freedom mean this   sparkling and I am not the shore
you are not the pool   I am not the drowning   I am writ-
ing this to you   in water   on water

4. *Wish you were here*

What the Water Holds

I exit the cabin door and leave the cabin
behind. The trail is covered over
by leaf litter, such a trashy name
for something so beautiful it ought
to be called leaf glitter. I stumble
on acorns and pinecones, catch
my footing on a raised root, fumble
into a nearby tree and hug it
then take a pushpin and leave a flyer
for a missing girl, because I am she.
I want you to find me but the photo
is years old and smudged. My hair is longer
and my cheeks are fuller and my jeans
so un-bedazzled. The birds eat the rhinestones
I've lost and now lay sparkly eggs.
The bears have taken up residence
in my cabin. I don't care. I should never
have been there, never have allowed myself
the usual comforts of home. I deserve only
what the water holds. It will hold me.
I will walk out to the water's edge
which is unpredictable and shallow.
Then I will wade into the lake and let
the water wash away my address, my name,
which you had written on my wrist
so I could find my way home.

Match

Show me the water, I will show you the milk.
We pair up and break down, upending.

The bridge is made of bread, greening & sinking.
The fruit floats, little berries head-bobbing.

My mouth in the water.
My mouth angling for the berry.

Nothing sustains us,
nothing as a substitute for air, for silence,

Silence the filling in of all that aches,
all that bobs in the water, lobbed to shore.

I am the bread, the milk.
I am the house on the edge, crumbling.

The birds have a habit of (not) helping.
I am the river, the birds.

Souring and blueing, the thick milk curdling.
I can't feed you the way I can

the feckless fox, the calculating rabbit.
I take your head, which is my own,

in my hands, in my lap: the house stills.
I massage the sand from between your ears,

wrong as the shallow waters that swallow
the young, the sweet-breathed milk-eaters that saw.

How we abandon ourselves to the wolves.
How we are ourselves the wolves.

I am the match, I am flammable.
God damn it all if I don't burn it down.

Because the Dead Are So Beautiful

We shield our eyes
from photographs, mirrors,
our own reflection.

Their beauty breaks us.
We are that fragile. We coax
mercy from ash, a light
dusting at cliffside.
Contrition laces
the milk of our days.

Tessellation of
heart-stars bursting.

Nurture these
delicate tinctures,
florid decay.

How to Teach a Cat to Type

1.
Put cat-
nip on
the keys
and let
said cat
roll on
the keys

2.
Stick
with
monosyllabic
words
at
first

3.
But of course,
one must start
by teaching
it to read

4.
Once she has mastered
Michel de Montaigne
move on to Schrödinger

5.
When she rejects
conventional
notions of
morality
be prepared to
accept the facts
as they evolve
to suit her

6.
If she asks for
a martini
("Up, dry,
with a mouse")
do not bring her
a gibson or
dirty, and by
no means should you
ever bring her
anything less
than top shelf

7.
Do not allow
her to wallow
in existential
crisis; instead,

remind her that
you long ago
swapped kibble for
squab and bring her
another drink

8.
When and/or if
she is ready
to begin, be
prepared to go
back to the beginning
and allow her
to rewrite
the instructions
herself

9.
If at that point
she chooses not
to, remember
Free Will, and forget
she was ever
just a cat

Novel

In the opening scene, the heroine (me) is hanging by her thumbs from a bridge. No, it is not meant to be comedic. My thumbs do not find this funny at all. As the camera pans wide you can see that the heroine (me) is dangling over a serene river. Yes, I know that rivers aren't serene. Okay, in this case, it is. Please bear with me. The river is gently flowing and her feet are almost touching down. Yes, I know that's a very low bridge. Anyway. She lets go and now she's in the river, except as you might have noticed before she's wearing a water-proof inflatable suit so that she's bobbing along with the current. Yes, it is kind of silly. Okay, then, I confess it is comedic, but on the other hand, if I were ever to choose to dangle from a bridge over a river by my thumbs, I would want to be prepared. I would wear a rubber suit, and maybe a snorkel, just in case. But back to my novel. Of course she's had to think through this because no one is there to save her. In fact, there are no crowds, and the cars on the road above just keep driving along. There is one lone stranger standing at the railing, looking down as she (I) float(s) beneath, from one side of the bridge to the other, in her (my) rubber inflatable suit. The stranger just watches, and then walks on. This is not so unusual, I think. We are all carried along by our own thoughts and sometimes we stop to watch but most times we can't be bothered. In the next scene, our heroine (I) swim(s) toward shore, where she (I) snag(s) a rock and the suit pops, but that's okay because she's on dry land now. She sheds the suit. There is no one waiting to help her from the water. She sits on the rocky shore. A car drives by, honks, waves, but not at her. In the final scene of the novel, she (I) stand(s), brushes herself off, goes home. The reader (you) seem to relate with her (me), in the way that sometimes a crisis feels a lot like falling into a river, and sometimes a river feels a lot like a wading pool, where the rubber ducks squeak and angel wings keep us afloat for the sequel.

Acknowledgments/Notes:

"A Gold Nothing and a Silver Wait-a-While" is a phrase my mother used, origin unknown.

"As Margaret Napped Through the Apocalypse" is forthcoming in BAM Writes 42-word story anthology, in a slightly different form.

"Because the Dead are So Beautiful" is in memory of the poet Julie Paegle.

"Evergreen" is based on a sad, movie-like dream from my childhood in which a boy turned into a checkerboard with Barbra Streisand singing in the background. The Robert Frost poem alluded to is "Nothing Gold Can Stay."

"Lazarus in the Bookstore" was inspired by meeting a real Lazarus in a real bookstore.

"Lofty" is after the painting "Tender Trapper" by Julie Heffernan.

"Match" originally appeared in *Mockingheart Review* and later in *The Body at a Loss*.

"Novel" originally appeared in *Hags on Fire*.

"Revival" originally appeared in *Pratik*, special double issue on Los Angeles poets.

"Richard Garcias are Everywhere" is after the poet Richard Garcia.

"Self-Portrait as the Wife with No Hands" previously published in *The Body, Like Bread*.

"Supernova, Or the End is Just the Beginning" is inspired in part by a quote from Thomas Stearns (T.S.) Eliot.

"The Apple-Polisher" is defined as "a person who behaves obsequiously to someone important" which has absolutely nothing to do with the poem.

"The Fish on the Floor" is an embodiment of a dream.

"The Door in the Forest" was an entry for *Rattle's* ekphrastic challenge and is after a painting by Åsa Antalffy Eriksson.

Many of these poems owe a debt to folklore scholarship, though none are based directly on any particular story.

About the Author

Cati Porter is the author of nine books and chapbooks, including most recently *Slow Unraveling of Living Ghosts*, a chapbook co-authored with Johnny Bender and with illustrations by Steve "Lu" Lossing. Her work has appeared in *So to Speak: A Feminist Journal of Language and Art*, as winner of their annual poetry competition, as well as many others including *Rattle, Verse Daily, Salon. com, Contrary, Shark Reef, West Trestle*, and *Pratik*. She lives in Inland Southern California with her family where she directs Inlandia Institute, a literary nonprofit.

BAMBOO DART PRESS

112 N. Harvard Ave. #65
Claremont, CA 91711
chapbooks@bamboodartpress.com
www.bamboodartpress.com

9 781947 240452